Legacy Begins with ME

MOTIVATING AND EMPOWERING WOMEN TO CREATE THEIR INHERITANCE

SIANTRA "CECE" GRAY

DEDICATION

This book is dedicated to my legacy: My sons, Aiden Isaiah-Rashaad and Ashton Israel-Rashaad, and any other children God sees fit to bestow upon me. I have made it my mission to build a life for you, one that will allow you to take advantage of every opportunity possible. I only hope I make you proud and inspire you to reach for more. You can do and achieve anything you put your mind to. Make it your mission to leave a legacy as I have attempted to leave for you.

To my support system: My amazing husband, Jeremy, my family and friends, THANK YOU! Thank you for your love, prayers, financial blessings, and encouraging words throughout this process. They helped to push me through more than you know.

This book is also dedicated to every woman who has impacted my life in some shape, form, or fashion. To those who have set the example and given me something to aspire to—because you did it, I knew that I could. To my first impact, my mom; I can never repay you, but I am definitely going to try! I love you!

TABLE OF CONTENTS

INTRODUCTION

Everyone in this world has a purpose, a reason for being. Whether you have children or not, we all have a legacy—a footprint in this earth that we must leave behind. One would assume that unfortunate circumstances from childhood would shape, and in many ways tarnish, the quality of your legacy. That is not always true. Yes, your childhood directly affects your success in adulthood, but it does not have to be negative.

Countless individuals have experienced trauma, heartbreak, and dysfunction, while others received the love and nurturing they always longed for. That does not mean that their beginnings determined their endings. Regardless of the canvas you were given to paint your life's story, you can always use tools obtained navigating through life and impartation to make your painting a beautiful masterpiece.

In this book, I share some of my experiences, lessons learned, trials and triumphs on my path to creating my inheritance—my legacy. Through it all, I share with you core principles on how to turn those circumstances into stepping stones, stones used to build and create your legacy. The scripture says, "All things work together for the good of them who love the Lord, and who are the called according to his purpose." God never spoils and never wastes. Nothing about you will be wasted, and guess what, it will be used for His glory.

It is my prayer that you are motivated and empowered to keep pushing, to keep building, not allowing "life" to make you give up or quit! There are people waiting on you to release what God has placed inside of you! As you read, be sure to notate and reflect on the legacy builders at the end of each chapter. Those will help you identify your areas of strength and opportunity. I have also included scriptures to meditate on at the end of each chapter. Feel free to write these out on index cards or sticky notes so that you can constantly recite them.

It is my prayer that my story will awaken something within you and push you to want more! It does not matter how your story starts; it matters most what you do to affect the ending. My legacy began with ME, and it is my job to Motivate and Empower you to understand that your Legacy begins with you. What will you do to affect generations to come?

1

BABY STEPS
ARE STILL PROGRESS

Ever since I can remember, I have aspired to become a doctor. I had some friends who went directly from undergraduate to medical school to residency with no problem. But there were also those who took a longer route to get there. Whether it was due to their GPA not being high enough, MCAT score not making the cut, or their inability to adequately stand out as much as the other phenomenal candidates; there always seemed to be a great level of opposition. This was my struggle. It seemed as if the harder I would try, the further my dream was from reality. I got married and birthed two children, which I am proud of, but it felt like those joyous occasions pushed my aspirations way down the line. It was not until I prayed about my current state and God's will for my life that I found peace.

We have our plan, and God has His plan. We must be okay with God's plan prevailing. Since being married and having my first son, I have also taken some courses in a post-baccalaureate medical program and obtained my master's. Am I where I want to be? No. But I am doing what I must do now (working full time, taking care of my family, and continuing to press educationally) until my time comes. Baby steps are still progress. Keep moving; keep striving; keep pushing towards that dream. It may not happen in your timing, but if it is a part of God's will for your life, it will happen.

Now, I must warn you that during this time of pushing forward you will become discouraged. You may run into people who were aware of your aspirations and ask, "Did you become a doctor yet?"

Or you may have those "accomplished" friends who ask, "What happened to you wanting to become a doctor?" yet in a condescending, what are you doing with your life tone. Statements like these can potentially send you into a downward spiral of depression. They did that to me. Every single time. You will start to regret decisions, most of which are blessings, and resent those things and people that you felt stood in your way. There are some who have the career but no one to share it with. I encourage you to take a step back and review the good, the beauty, and the blessings in your life. In reality, many may want the very things you have. You may not be where you thought you would be, but know that you are indeed blessed beyond measure.

Legacy Scripture: Being confident of this very thing, that he which hath begun a good work in you will perform it until the day of Jesus Christ - (Philippians 1:6).

Legacy Builder: What are some goals/aspirations that you are working towards?

How are you working to get them accomplished?

2

DON'T BE AFRAID
TO ASK FOR HELP

I am a very independent person. I have always been taught to be strong, stay focused, and make it happen; whatever "it" may be. My mother always found a way to provide everything I needed, even if it took her working two jobs every day - or planning to have me by her side at these jobs so she wouldn't have to bother anyone. Whatever had to be done, she found a way to make things work with ease.

Seeing this as a child made me a no-nonsense type of person. If I was struggling, had no money, and no way to eat that night, no one would know it. I made sure my bills were paid, and, to me, that is all that mattered. Though this is a good trait to have, it was and is not always healthy. Yes, you want to be self-sufficient and not dependent on people for everything, but you must also decipher when you need help.

As a mommy, working full time, still trying to progress educationally and find additional streams of income, it gets hard. You try to "Be Here Now" with your little ones, be the best wife ever, mature in your relationship and time spent with God, give your all at work so you can win a promotion, keep your home clean, have dinner prepared, clothes washed and ironed for the week, be present and available for family and friends who need you; it can all be overwhelming! Then you find yourself upset with your spouse because he/she is not helping. You realize you haven't asked for help! And even when you do, you come right behind them and do it your way.

Friend, let me be the first to tell you, it is okay to ask for help. I encourage you to learn how to ask for help, even when you feel like you have it all together. These bodies get tired and weary all the time. Learn how to delegate to other people and be okay with it not being done exactly as you would do it. Don't be a control freak like I was. Don't suffer in silence because your pride won't let you ask for help. It doesn't make you weak, dependent, or less of a person—it makes you human.

I'm extremely organized, most times, and try to do everything to perfection, but I've concluded that things won't always be perfect. If you can deal with that, and be okay with others helping, especially when a new addition comes along, you will find yourself happier, at peace, and more peaceful with others. Everyone will thank you for it. And if you are the person offering help, let me extend a little word of advice. Don't offer your assistance then complain the entire time. That will make the person never ask for help again, which is counterproductive. Assist with a happy, willing heart.

Legacy Scripture: If you need wisdom, ask our generous God, and He will give it to you. He will not rebuke you for asking - (James 1:5).

Legacy Builder: What are some areas you could be a little more hands-off?

Why is it so hard for you to ask for help?

What else could you get accomplished if you had consistent help?

3

LEARN TO LISTEN

I was what you called a smart girl in school—top of my class, always made good grades, and, like most, I thought I knew it all. As I matriculated through undergrad, I realized something about myself. I listened with the intent to respond. This means that I listened only enough to formulate a comeback or "smart response." It wasn't until God connected me with one of my role models/mentors that I learned to truly listen.

This lady did not take any mess. Anything she saw, she called me out on it. She would get on to me so much that I started to think she really did not like me. I always felt personally attacked and could not understand why she kept me around.

One day, I decided that I was going to take a nonchalant approach. I started to act as if nothing she said bothered me. It wasn't until I let my guard down and removed my ability to be offended that I listened and internalized what she was saying. All this time, what I took as fussing were droplets of wisdom. From how I carried myself to what I wore; from how I behaved at a guest's home to my body language, this lady taught me how to be the young lady I am today. And I am still learning from her. How much further along would I be had I learned to listen from the beginning and not be so defensive? How many blessings and connections have we missed because our ears were closed? There is a difference between hearing and actually listening.

Though this was a positive situation that I experienced, there have been some negative ones as well. I have had people who were speaking into my life, but they were not speaking blessings. They were knowingly sending me down a path of destruction. This is why it is important to be in tune with God because He will let you know which connections are not healthy, if you listen. It is imperative to be sensitive to God's leading to distinguish between those who are speaking life into you and those who are acting as serpents. Yes, we must learn to listen, but I've also been taught how to eat the meat and spit out the bones. Take evaluation. Listen to those around you and figure out who is for you, building you, and helping you to mature. All others can be removed. In this season, we are moving forward. Learn to listen to God's leading and the voice of wisdom spoken through those who want to see you succeed.

Legacy Scripture: Understand this, my dear brothers and sisters: You must all be quick to listen, slow to speak, and slow to get angry. Human anger does not produce the righteousness God desires. So, get rid of all the filth and evil in your lives, and humbly accept the word God has planted in your hearts, for it has the power to save your souls. But don't just listen to God's word. You must do what it says. Otherwise, you are only fooling yourselves - (James 1:19–22).

Legacy Builder: Are there areas of your life in which you could listen more and talk less?

Who are the mentors in your life?

How can you identify those placed in your life to push you toward your destiny?

4

WATCH YOUR ENVIRONMENT

How many of you have heard the phrase "Birds of a Feather Flock Together?" I'm sure we all have. In some instances, we felt like it was true, while in others, we didn't. This phrase was always used in a negative light when I was little. Adults would use it to describe young ladies that I did not need to surround myself with, as they were considered to be "fast" or too grown for their age. I felt that I was different and set apart because I was not easily influenced. Just because one person did something, that did not mean that I would do it as well.

As I got older, I understood that this statement also had a positive side to it. I noticed that successful people hung around other successful people. This is when I learned to watch my environment and surround myself, not only with like-minded individuals, but those who were where I was trying to get to. In undergrad, I learned to study with those who could help explain a topic to me, not those who were barely passing biochemistry like me. I tried my best to watch those I kept in my circle and make sure my environment was conducive for growth, not remaining stagnant. I had to envelop myself with people who would encourage and push me but also tell me when I was off focus and needed to get it together. Even if I did not feel like I could be the biggest asset to them, in that particular season, I never forgot to do my part in some way to show my gratitude and appreciation.

While attempting to clear the clutter of your environment, you will have those who talk about you, say that you think you are better than them or act like you are too good to be around them. Don't let this bother you or discourage you. There are some people we are to remain connected to as lights in their lives, but then there are others who will begin to remove themselves from your life. This is okay. Don't stand in the way. Allow it to happen. As people move out of your life/space at the end of one season, others will move in to help propel you to where you need to be. Embrace change and watch your environment. Stay around people who are moving forward, who can pour into you and challenge you to be the best you possibly can be.

Legacy Scripture: Oh, the joys of those who do not follow the advice of the wicked, or stand around with sinners, or join in with mockers. 2.But they delight in the law of the Lord, meditating on it day and night. 3.They are like trees planted along the riverbank, bearing fruit each season. Their leaves never wither, and they prosper in all they do - (Psalm 1:1–3).

Legacy Builder: Are there things and people in your life causing you to be stagnant?

Who have you connected with who is there to push, build you, and hold you accountable?

5

TALK & EXPRESS, DON'T INTERNALIZE

I have heard this remark countless times! I am not one who responds quickly or blows up on the spur of the moment. I think; I analyze; I internalize. Sometimes it is a blessing and a curse. Thinking before speaking allows you to pick your words, responses, and actions carefully but, more importantly, ensure you won't be embarrassed by your behavior or words while upset.

I have been the victim of a lot of words that have cut deep, whether the individual meant for that to be the result or not. Hearing as a child, "You're going to end up pregnant like your mother," forced me to try harder to ensure that statement never came to pass. To hear, "Your daddy ain't no good," sent me on a quest as a teen to find a man who would treat me the exact opposite. Whether words are spoken to a person's face in the heat of battle, uttered in disgust because you were the byproduct of someone else's mistake, or overheard by a room of adults who had a little too much to drink, words hurt.

We have often heard the phrase, "People may not remember what you did, but they remember how you made them feel." Individuals grow and they mature, but feelings seem to take a little longer. I even realized at one point that these words and opinions were my sole driving forces to be successful. But were those real reasons?

Before I got married, my husband and I attended pre-marital counseling. This was a time to find out who you are really marrying; you know, the real you, not your representative! Lol! In counseling, they stressed the importance of sharing what is on your mind and in your heart, and often. Be honest. Be real.

Simply put, communicate. Communication, or should I say effective communication, has been known to be a missing key component in many failed relationships and marriages. If you are anything like me, and you finally get to the point where you are 100% open, share your feelings, pour out your heart, and nothing changes, you make sure you do not do that again. It is like the person didn't hear a word you said. This in turn causes you not to open yourself up or be vulnerable again. My dear friend, let me tell you that you can't always do this. This goes for males and females. It is a defense mechanism personally set up to rob you of your ability to feel or deal. This aids in your continual cycle of going through life unfulfilled and unhappy. Ask me how I know.

One thing I have learned and am continuing to learn is that people have their own timing and way of dealing with things, just like you do. You cannot be upset with others because they communicate differently from you, though you can work together to come to a mutual understanding and effective form of communication. Realize that open dialogue is needed. Just because someone responds to feelings you may express or- tries to bring clarity to the situation -does not mean that your feelings are discounted. It does not mean they do not care. It means they are attempting to have a conversation about your feelings. Don't shut down or play the victim role, like no one ever listens to you. Listening is a must, but don't expect people to listen without a single response. Express with an intent to listen, understand, and fix the situation. Internalizing can cause bitterness, built-up anger, and un-fulfillment of unrealistic or unspoken expectations that were never discussed. Though silence is beneficial at times, it can also serve as a distraction, a robber of joy, time, and focus. Talk. Discuss how you feel. Speak up. Express yourself. It is okay to take a moment to gather yourself and your emotions, but don't take too long. You will feel better and won't have to wonder "what if?" I don't mean pop off, because sometimes the way we say things affect how they are received and acted upon. Think, consider your responses, and move accordingly.

With this new perspective, be aware that people will try you and try to push your buttons. Throw a curveball in there and change the way you respond. Your limits may be known by those trying to embarrass you or make you act out of character, but you have a secret weapon called self-control. Use it often! Show growth and maturity. You cannot control the actions of others, but you can control how you respond. Don't embarrass yourself.

Legacy Scripture: My mouth shall speak wisdom, And the meditation of my heart shall give understanding - (Psalm 49:3).

Legacy Builder: In which areas can you communicate better?

What have you been holding in?

How can your change in responses aid in building your relationships?

At what point do you stop talking and just move on?

6

TRUST

Trust has been a problem area for me for years. I am not sure the exact source of it, but it grabbed hold of me at a very young age. My biological father, though I'm sure he meant well, was a man of broken promises. Whether it was money for a trip or showing up for something important at school, if he said he would do it, I believed him. Unfortunately, the ending of that was usually tears and me asking my mom why I wasn't important enough to keep a simple promise. There was always a good story or reason why, and after a while, I just became numb and stopped asking, stopped expecting, and stopped trying. Trust as I knew it was out the door for me. I did not believe people when they said things. My favorite motto was, "I'll believe it when I see it."

I remember being in a store with my godmother around Christmas time. She was picking out Christmas gifts for her ministry team, who had given their time and energy all year. As I was helping her, she told me to pick out something I wanted. I froze in shock and really did not think I heard her correctly. This was the very first time I had experienced someone's kindness "just because." There had to be a motive. She had not given me a reason not to trust her, but because I was so damaged and wounded in the area of trust, I had to be reprogrammed. The very people I trusted growing up hurt me, lied to me, and tried to take advantage of me, and all of that unfortunately led to molestation and rape. Some people can be so damaged mentally and emotionally that they begin to believe that these interactions were their fault.

The enemy is something else because this is far from the truth. This is not love and your trust should never be violated.

When I first met my husband, I would not give him the time of day. He literally stalked me! I did not know what he wanted, why he liked me, what his motives were, etc. I did not trust, especially males; however, after much prayer and guidance, I finally gave him a chance. Ladies, we can be so hurt and damaged that we push away the very answer to prayer that God has sent our way. I love hard and I will give my last, but I had not learned how to receive that from others, with no strings attached. I remember telling my husband before we started dating, "I'll trust you until you give me a reason not to, so please do not violate my trust."

Now I am learning how to trust again, once trust has been broken. That seems like one of the toughest things in the world to me. Having trust issues can spill over into other areas of your life so beware. Don't tarnish relationships and God-ordained connections because of your lack of trust and ability to let go and move on. I am not saying you should allow people to walk all over you, but be open enough to allow God to bless you through others. Learn to trust and trust again. Some of your biggest opportunities may come by trusting someone you do not know, who could put you in the presence of great men. After all, put yourself on the other side of it; if you messed up, you would want someone to not only forgive but trust you again.

Legacy Scripture: But blessed are those who trust in the Lord and have made the Lord their hope and confidence - (Jeremiah 17:7).

But when I am afraid, I will put my trust in you. I praise God for what he has promised. I trust in God, so why should I be afraid" - (Psalm 56:3–4).

Legacy Builder: What are some areas in which you could do better in trusting others?

What doors are you allowing to close because you trust your understanding and logic more than God?

How can you learn to trust again?

7

LET GO OF THE PAST & PRESS FORWARD

On my mother's side, I am the oldest of three children; 14 of those years, I was an only child. I absolutely love being the big sister to my sister and brother. Yet, many were the days that I longed to have a big sister or close sibling I could confide in. I had cousins, I had close friends, but our bond did not seem to reach that inseparable level, like that of siblings.

On my biological father's side, I believe I am the middle child. There was some question as to whether I was the only girl, but that is neither here nor there. My siblings and stepsister seemed to have a tighter bond with my father than I did. Their memories are somehow drastically different from mine. I was never a "Daddy's girl," and at times felt as if I was the stepchild. I longed to have that bond and relationship, not only with my father but with my siblings. For some reason, we were just different, or at least I felt isolated as different. And after experiencing a period of abuse, confusion, and mental anguish within myself, I believe that distance never repaired. I stayed away from revisiting anything that reminded me of that dark place I was in at that stage of my life, if I could.

I quickly noticed that the feelings of isolation and loneliness were not only present in those relationships but also in my friendships. I could not understand how I could be an amazing friend and confidante to some but never get that in return. I did not understand how I could give of myself and my time and it go unnoticed. I probably shouldn't reveal this, but I even considered pledging in undergrad because I deeply desired to have that tight bond of love, growth, and friendship but more importantly uniformity in purpose; this was something I longed for and lacked. I have seen some awesome ladies become like sisters, dropping everything to be at the aid of the person they did not know existed a few months prior. It was because they went through and experienced things together that formed that relationship. Who was my go-to person? Who would be there no matter what? You know Mom will always be there. Parents will be there. But who is there when you can't call them? Who do you tell your secrets to? My reality was I could not answer those questions.

Experiencing these thoughts as a child, or even young adult, can mess with your mind. There was a period when I found myself down and depressed. Why did I grow up the way I did? Why was I court-ordered to visits between my mother and father every other weekend? Why was I subject to two different lifestyles? Why did I always feel like the shape that didn't fit? Why did I experience loneliness, sadness, and anger all at the same time? Why was I taken advantage of sexually to the point that I felt there was no way out other than death? These were questions that would plague my mind every single day. Yes, this honor student and aspiring medical doctor was on a downward spiral at 100 mph.

I knew if I was going to come out of this thing alive, if I was going to be anything in life, I had to stop asking myself those self-inflicted, woe-is-me questions. I was not who I wanted to be and knew there was more to life for me than what I had experienced. After all, I was going to be the change in my family. I always felt a pulling, a tugging, a drawing of something bigger than myself, but I never knew what. But in order to find out, I had to let go of the past and press forward. I could not continue to ask myself the same questions repeatedly. They were and are my reality, but if I was going to change the trajectory of my future, I had to get it together and fast! If I was going to experience the fullness of what God had in store for me, I had to let go and press forward.

So what I did not come from a line of wealth? I had parents who loved me and tried their best to provide for me. So what I felt like I was a real-life chameleon growing up? It allowed me to remain humble and stay focused on the change I aspired to be. Little did I know, others wished they were in my shoes. So what I did not grow up with someone to tell all of my secrets to? I learned how to build a relationship with God, discern His voice, and He in turn connected me with three amazing women, who are my godmothers today. They have taught me, poured into me, prayed over me, chastised me, and the list can go on and on. They saw something in me that I could not see in myself. My mom and granny were great examples, and I'm grateful that God thought enough of me to send all the help He could. And since then, I have been able to share that same help with others of all ages. But in order to receive, in order to see with spiritual eyes and not natural eyes, in order to step into the new path that was set before me I had to let go of the past and press forward.

And the same is true for you. You cannot dwell on where life has taken you or the lack thereof. No longer can you be distracted or haunted by your past. Stop hindering yourself by continuously revisiting that place of pain and discomfort. Face it head-on, deal with it, get healing, get counseling, whatever you feel like you need to do, because your future depends on it. There is a group of people on this earth waiting on you to step into your purpose. Are you going to keep them waiting? Of course not. Let go of the past and press forward. Don't just move forward; press with intention, with focus, with purpose.

Legacy Scripture: I'm not saying that I have this all together, that I have it made. But I am well on my way, reaching out for Christ, who has so wondrously reached out for me. Friends, don't get me wrong: By no means do I count myself an expert in all of this, but I've got my eye on the goal, where God is beckoning us onward—to Jesus. I'm off and running, and I'm not turning back - (Philippians 3:12–14).

Legacy Builder: What situations or people are you holding on to?

Have you forgiven yourself for being distracted by hurt and remaining stagnant?

Write out a plan that will ensure you continue to press forward and don't fall back into the past.

8

YOU'VE GOTTEN AN APOLOGY, NOW WHAT?

November 29, 2014 is a day I will never forget. My husband and I lived in Dallas at the time and decided to visit home for Thanksgiving. I was pregnant with our first son, Aiden, and we thought it would be convenient to have a baby shower during this trip. After all, having family and friends there to celebrate seemed to make the occasion a little more real and joyous.

During my shower, I was informed by a family member that my father was in a nursing home/rehab center. A few health challenges had overtaken him, and by this time, his leg had been amputated and he was blind. I do not know what prompted me to, but I decided to go visit him after the shower. I had not seen him in a long time and really did not know what to expect.

It seemed as if the closer we drove to the location, the smaller I became. It was like I was reverting to this little girl that only wanted to be loved, supported, and appreciated by her father. Regardless of the mistakes, the disappointments, the broken promises, and flat-out lies, none of that seemed to matter now.

When my husband and I arrived, my stepmother greeted us with a hug and her warm smile. She explained to my father that I was there, but unfortunately, he could only go off his memory of what I looked like. He was not able to see my big, round belly and slightly full face. He was not able to see my amazingly handsome husband, nor was he able to see my mother, his battle partner for the majority of my life. He spoke to me, asked how I was, how life had been, and then proceeded to apologize. He apologized for everything. Everything. I am not sure if anyone else there realized what was happening in those moments or if they chalked it up to him being emotional and happy because his daughter had come to see him.

"I'm sorry." "I apologize." It's amazing how those two little phrases can have such a great impact on a person. Did all my hurt and pain go away in that instant? No! I never realized how many "voided areas" I carried into my adulthood and, ultimately, into my marriage. But I felt something break at that moment. I realized that it was up to me at this point to let it go. I was starting a family of my own and had to start building my own legacy. I could not dwell on the past any longer. How do you dwell on something someone has already apologized for? You can't. You must work through your own healing process and find a way not to repeat the same cycle you felt you were trapped in.

Something deep within me knew that would be the last time I would see my father alive. If I did not visit him and have that moment on that day; if I was too stubborn, hurt, or just did not care to go and see him on that day, I cannot say how I would feel. I would add to the list of countless "What if" questions I already had.

My father passed away a few weeks before I gave birth to our son. I was too far along to travel back home, so I attended the funeral via Facetime. I had so many mixed emotions, coupled with a shattered reality. That week was probably one of the most challenging weeks of my life, but one thing was for sure; I was closing that chapter of my life and moving forward. After all, those two phrases were still echoing in my mind and in my heart. We have no idea why God allows things to happen the way they do. We just trust His will and plans for our lives. Though I still have my moments, I don't dwell there long, because I must remain focused.

I admonish you, my friend, to do the same thing. Maybe there are obstacles that seemed to set you back. Maybe there were promises that were never fulfilled. Maybe there were relationships that were never mended. But, guess what. Holding on to them does not change the reality of them. Your response holds you hostage. Free yourself today. Free your mind, your heart, and your emotions. One of the most important things you can do is grieve. I did not learn this until recently. I never grieved my father's death until recently. I didn't know I needed to. But I had to grieve his loss and grieve the reality that the relationship that I longed to have will never come to pass. Grieve the loss, grieve what was, but also grieve and release your ties to what will never be. Give God all your broken pieces and allow Him to not only heal you but make you whole.

Legacy Scripture: Have compassion on me, Lord, for I am weak. Heal me, Lord, for my bones are in agony. I am sick at heart. How long, O Lord, until you restore me? - (Psalms 6:2–3).

O Lord, if you heal me, I will be truly healed; if you save me, I will be truly saved. My praises are for you alone - (Jeremiah 17:14).

Legacy Builder: Take a moment and mentally revisit some areas of hurt and pain in your life. What are these areas?

Have you forgiven those who hurt you, even without apology?

What are your plans to facilitate a healthy healing process and who can assist you through it?

9

RENEW YOUR MIND

Amid writing this book, I went through periods of not writing. When I sat down to write, nothing was there. No thoughts, no inspiration, nothing. There was so much going on around me that I was not in a frame of mind or mental state to write. To be completely transparent, I felt like my life was crumbling all around me. I found myself in a place of complacency at work, unfulfilled and ready to move on, trying to make changes and prepare for a newborn at home and battle with issues within my marriage, which I am sure every couple experiences. How could I write and be inspirational to others, giving them hope and motivation, if I lacked it myself? There is a such thing as pouring out to the point of drought, and I think I had reached that place.

Even my safe haven, which in a sense was church, was going through changes. I had stopped everything I loved doing: teaching, directing, ministering, etc. I basically found myself at a standstill in every area of my life. The only constant was this little man I was carrying, growing fast and quickly approaching his due date. I knew for my own sanity and to make sure I was "fixed" before the baby arrived, I had to do something. I had to go back to what I knew. I had to double my prayer time, watch the food I was intaking, increase my worship time, be intentional about the music I listened to, remind myself of my goals and how I planned to complete them, and, most importantly, I had to get some rest.

To be honest, I had to take a step back and realize that I was in a different place mentally, emotionally, physically, spiritually, basically in every aspect. I had to give myself a little grace, recognizing and acknowledging the fact that I was currently growing a little human inside of me. I needed rest. I needed to take it easy if I did not want to put myself or this little miracle at risk. I needed to be more patient with myself and with my current state. No, things were not what I wanted them to be at this point, but they would never be what is needed to move forward if I didn't take a step back and rebuild my foundation. I realized that I was preparing for a new normal, and a new normal requires change, adjustment, and refocus. A mental check was in order; one where I faced my reality and planned for my future. How could I start a new career on a shaky foundation? How could I build my marriage if we weren't on the same page? How could I know where to go to feed my spirit if I was not in tune with God without distraction?

Building requires a firm foundation and sometimes that means taking a step back to observe all aspects of a situation. If you are at this point, don't be embarrassed. You would be surprised how many people suffer in silence. Oftentimes, those who seem like they have it all together are the most broken, either because they do not have anyone to confide in or because they do not understand that facing reality is not the end. I almost did not write about this myself, but then I told myself even the strongest people go through it. Even the toughest people go through hard times. What makes you different from everyone else who experiences this is you are willing to do whatever it takes to get back on track. When you fall, when you feel like you are not progressing forward, when you feel like all hell is breaking loose, tell yourself it will be okay.

People will try you in this season. They will even judge you and try to continuously remind you of your "rough seasons." Don't get upset with them and don't allow that to get you down or depressed. Stay focused and know that you are stronger and better because you went through hard times. You are more appreciative, more in tune with God, and more focused on the goal at hand. Be intentional about giving God the best and most of you. Once He is in line where He should be, then things will get in balance and in line, including your mindset. Once your mindset has shifted and is renewed, Press Forward.

Legacy Scripture: Don't copy the behavior and customs of this world, but let God transform you into a new person by changing the way you think. Then you will learn to know God's will for you, which is good and pleasing and perfect - (Romans 12:2).

Legacy Builder: When was the last time you took a step back to evaluate where you are in life?

What things or people are holding you hostage to your past and won't allow you to progress forward?

How can you recognize and avoid these distractions in the future?

10

WHO ARE YOU AT YOUR CORE?

Growing up, I always felt the pressure to be the best. I felt like I had to make the best grades, have nice clothes, be involved in the community, etc. I just always felt the weight of "expectations" that people had of me, whether they verbalized them or made sly statements comparing me to others. One thing about expectations, before you know it you will start to become that thing people are expecting you to become. That pressure can be so stressful that you lose sight of who you really are. It's easy to lose you when you are more concerned with who everyone expects you to be. Because I didn't feel like I had the freedom to express myself, my feelings, or what I was dealing with, I had this strong shell. In my mind, this shell protected my heart and my emotions. No one could get in. After all, I was expected to be the one who had it all together. Behind that shell was hurt, pain, guilt, regret, anger, and confusion. So many emotions that I could not express or explain. One thing I learned the hard way: if you keep all these things in, you will make yourself either physically sick or mentally crazy.

It wasn't until I moved away to undergrad and found myself completely alone at night that I had to face my reality. How could I pick friends at college if I didn't even know who I was? Little did I know, all those things I suppressed years before, behind my shell, would all come bursting out in ways I did not expect.

In search of the real me, I found myself deep in my Bible but also searching. I was searching for things to fill voids that I had in my life. Whether it was the feeling of being loved or having friends so close that we felt like the sisters I never had, I was searching. I found myself working two jobs while matriculating through undergrad, just so I would not have to face that person in the mirror. I stayed busy and on-the-go so I would not feel.

One day, while away at Vanderbilt University, I got the worst migraine. I took medicine but it did not help. I woke up with bloodshot streaks through my eyes where blood vessels had burst. I found myself under the covers, in bed for days. I would try to go to class, but as soon as I stood up, I would be met with anxiety and sickness. I could not explain what was happening to me, but I knew it wasn't good. I was stressed, emotionally drained, and mentally absent. I had been struggling to achieve the goal of becoming a doctor while failing both chemistry and calculus. I could not deal with the pressure of not achieving. I could not be a disappointment. It got so bad physically that I was forced to take a semester off from school. How could I explain this to my parents? I couldn't. I told them I was fine because I could not introduce them to the person behind the mask. That person, in my eyes, had become a failure.

Little did I know, this was the beginning of my healing process. This time, there were no distractions, no busyness, nothing but me, on my face, crying out to God, asking Him to heal my heart, my mind, and, more importantly, heal me from disappointing myself. It wasn't until I gave my expectations over to God that He began to direct my path. Before now, though I said God was leading me, He wasn't. Pleasing people was leading me. Being who they wanted me to be was ruling me. By this time, I had been molested, raped, confused, just every emotion you could think of, and only a few people knew it. I was in search of a father's love I never felt like I got. I craved a mother's time and bond that I never felt like I got. I was longing for a sister's confidence that I never felt like I had. It was time for me to stop focusing on the wrong and focus on the right. At my core, I found out who I was and what I was made of. I found out what I liked, what made me happy, things I had never taken the time to find out. I learned areas that I struggled in and areas that I needed growth and maturity in.

Once you get tired of being tired, you will free yourself of the bondage you put yourself in. We all have circumstances. We all have unfortunate events that have affected us one way or another, but we cannot allow those things to rule our minds, our thoughts, our actions, or our overall being. Sadly, there are people who still haven't found out who they are at their core. Maybe you have to be like me and get in prayer or sit down and write out who you are, what you want in life, etc. It will help you get back on the right track.

Now I have a loving husband. Whenever I need a reminder, those two little men of mine remind me that they love me by their random slobbery kisses or unexpected hugs. I didn't have that sister's love, but now I have the awesome responsibility of being the sister I wanted. I have a "dad" that I can call on anytime, known as PawPaw to my sons. And my mom and I have a bond/understanding on a level I can't articulate. Thanks be to God for showing me who I am, so I can successfully be who I need to be in the lives of others. Who is waiting on you to walk in your divine purpose? Check your core.

Legacy Scripture: Thou wilt keep him in perfect peace, whose mind is stayed on thee: because he trusteth in thee - (Isaiah 26:3).

Legacy Builder: Who are you at your core?

Who are you unconsciously trying to please?

How much do you know about yourself?

11

ESTABLISH YOUR VILLAGE

We all need people around us who look out for our best interest. We need those friends who can take a step back and see the big picture, even when we cannot see it ourselves. No matter what job you have, how much money you have, or where you go in life, you need a "village." This village can be family, friends, role models, anyone. Your village doesn't have to be large, but it does need to include someone who can speak life into you; someone who can help recalibrate and refocus your mind; someone who can encourage you and one who makes sure you never forget to laugh. We all need those people who can remind us of those things we once knew but somehow forgot.

Recently, I was going through a rough situation. I had come to my wits' end and I made up my mind that I simply was not going to deal with it anymore. I felt like I deserved better in the situation and was tired of getting less than that. I knew what I was promised and refused to settle. One of my good friends, who is more like a sister, was able to help me get my mind focused on things that mattered more than how I "felt" in that moment.

Not only did she look at the situation with an unbiased view, she began to quote scripture after scripture, helping me to apply the Word to the situation. If you don't have a friend like this, you are missing out! I was amazed by her ability to hear my heart, sympathize with me, and yet not leave me there. My mood was brought up by every word she reminded me of. My faith and my expectations came up as well. I was able to leave feeling fulfilled, grateful, and finding myself "content in whatever situation I found myself in."

Remember to always give thanks in everything, for in that, you are in the will of God. Whether I like the situation or not, I must be grateful and give thanks because it is there that I am in the will of God and in His plan for my life. It may not look like it, but all things really do work together for the good. My current feelings, my tears, my frustration are all working for my good. The growth that will result from this trial, and the next, is working for my good. The changes I need to make in my perception and attitude towards the situation are working for my good.

I know for a fact that God put me on her heart that day, and I am forever grateful to Him for sending her my way. Establish a village that will not allow you to settle, be mediocre, or live below your potential. If these people are for you and connected to your purpose, they will stop at nothing to see you operating right where you are supposed to be. And don't just be the recipient, but be the person on the other side as well who encourages, uplifts, motivates, and reminds others that they can make it another day. I always receive these gentle reminders that God has not forgotten about me and is listening. That is the best reassurance I can ask for. Your village may change over time, but, in that, make sure you maintain people who can assist you in achieving purpose.

Legacy Scripture: Where there is no counsel, the people fall; But in the multitude of counselors there is safety - (Proverbs 11:14).

Legacy Builder: Who does your village consist of?

Are you surrounded by people who can speak life into you?

How do you know when it is time to re-establish your village?

12

START TODAY

I have wanted to write a book for years. I felt like God allowed me to experience things at a young age to help others down the line. I would always think about what I would say, what kind of audience I wanted to appeal to, and the countless lives that would be impacted from me sharing my heart and experiences. But for some reason, I just never sat down to start anything. People are all talk. They can have great ideas, but, unfortunately, very few of them actually step out and do the necessary things to make it happen.

I fell into this category myself. I would put off doing what I knew was in my heart to do. It felt like I had unending strength when it came to supporting and pushing others towards their destiny, but as soon as I took time to sit and focus on mine, I would become overwhelmingly tired or too mentally drained to focus on it. I had to have a reality check with myself and get it together. If you won't take the time to invest in you, why should others? How can you expect someone to financially sow into your life, dreams, and goals if you can't put your phone down long enough to build your legacy? It is a harsh reality, but it is the truth.

Rarely does success just fall into your lap. Wealth and finances are simply given to some because of their bloodline, but it is not the case for most people. Those who are truly successful have put in long, hard hours, building their brand, trying to create a legacy and life for those who come behind them. My godmother always says, "Do what you have to do now, so you can do what you want to do later." This statement has always stuck with me. If I know what it feels like to struggle, why not put in a little extra work to ensure those behind me don't experience the same thing? You may not have a bright idea that will change the world, or business connections that line you up for a multi-million-dollar business, but guess what. You can start today with the small things you have. Start a blog, be consistent with encouraging posts, make keepsakes to sell; any gift or talent you have, share it. I have often heard that the things that bring you great joy, pleasure, and enjoyment can also be the very area God uses to bring you into great wealth. On the flip side of that, the things that grieve and frustrate you the most may give insight into your purpose.

What is stopping you from starting today? The same thing that will stop you tomorrow, next week, in three months, and before you know it, an entire year has passed, and you are still "waiting to start." A year in which you could have been one step closer to your destiny. You could have made a little extra money. You definitely could have made a few more connections had you just taken the leap and started ... today. Don't let another month or year of reflection make you realize what you have missed out on. The worst thing you could do is not try.

So, what are you about to do now? Take out a piece of paper and write out your game plan. Start today. Write the intro to that book. Register for that LLC status. Purchase that space and turn it into something amazing. Do it! Today! Nothing is stopping you but you. Don't worry about money; don't worry about help. Worry about how you will keep up once God starts blessing that vision!

Legacy Scripture: Now you should finish what you started. Let the eagerness you showed in the beginning be matched now by your giving. Give in proportion to what you have. Whatever you give is acceptable if you give it eagerly. And give according to what you have, not what you don't have - (2 Corinthians 8: 11–12).

Legacy Builder: What is in your heart that you have been putting off?

Take a moment and think about these things. Write them out and plan how to execute them.

You may not have all the answers, but you have a start!

13

REFINE YOUR REFLECTION

We all have dreams and goals in life. Some of us have had visions of what our lives would be like, even as a young child. What job you would have, who you would marry, your dream wedding, home, children, etc. It is not until reality does not resemble this vision that we get down, off focus, and troubled. Dreams are sometimes not reality, and that is okay.

I remember when I was about 10, I said I would start saving money for my dream wedding. I knew that day would be magical, and I did not want anyone to tell me, "No," to anything I wanted for that day. As I grew older and was exposed to different things, I resolved that I no longer wanted to be married. In essence, I did not need to save money for that purpose anymore. Maybe I could enjoy a nice trip or purchase something nice for myself after undergrad, but my initial reasoning for saving had changed. I no longer wanted to be married. It was too hard. Too much work for nothing in return. Who I was and who I thought I wanted to be had changed. So I thought.

God saw fit to connect me with an amazing couple who had me reconsider this marriage thing. I liked what I saw in their marriage. Was it perfect? No, but it worked. They were great parents. They supported each other, worked together to make sure both of their goals were accomplished; they challenged one another intellectually, it just seemed like something I wanted in my future. I had this perfect person in my mind—I actually wrote out the qualities I wanted my husband to have. While many were superficial, some were real deal-breakers. After finishing my long list, I had to ask myself, *Now, what qualities do you bring to the table?* I sat there in silence for a moment. I had to really think about this question. Not what I thought were the best things about me but what someone who would spend the rest of their lives with me would say.

I realized that I would be taking more baggage into my marriage than positives. I had trust issues stemming from my relationship, or the lack thereof, with my father. I had low self-esteem from lacking affirmation from the people I needed it from most. I felt like I needed to amaze people and fit in, which stemmed from being an only child for most of my life and wanting that best friend in a sibling. There were so many things I needed to work on to match or even be compatible with that person I wrote on paper. Not once did I seek God about the person I would marry. I told God that he needed to be everything I wrote down, like I knew best. The most important thing I could do was to work on me. I needed to refine the person I saw in the mirror and the person I reflected to others. I had to ask myself, *Who do others see when they see me? Do they see broken pieces? Do they see the person who thinks they have it all together because of their accomplishments to date?* I knew that whoever I married, I had to be completely open and honest with them about my past, about my experiences, and make sure they agreed to the task of being patient while I figured it out. I felt if I could come into the marriage open, honest, and transparent, and they still loved me, then I could do the same.

We must always remember to work on us. Oftentimes we are quick to see what others lack and where they need help. We compare ourselves to others and think we make matters better by saying we aren't as bad as the next person. What does that accomplish? Nothing. We are all works in progress, and we all need to remember what we look like in the mirror. Do you like who or what you see when you look in the mirror? If you don't, what are you doing to refine this reflection? Do you reflect love? Do you reflect forgiveness? Do you reflect encouragement to others? Be the person you would want to encounter and interact with, especially if you claim to be a child of God. His reflection should be what we strive for. Daily, our goal should be to be more like Him, in every aspect. Will we be perfect? Absolutely not, but it is the heart and the pursuit of Him that gets His attention. Never stop pursuing that reflection.

Legacy Scripture: Instead, let the Spirit renew your thoughts and attitudes. Put on your new nature, created to be like God- truly righteous and holy - (Ephesians 4:23–24).

Legacy Builder: Would you consider yourself a light in the lives of others?

How can you continuously refine your reflection?

Do you like your reflection?

14

HAVE A PLAN

Sometimes I wish I was a child again. Our imaginations were so vast and in our minds we could do absolutely anything. That is until we were met with something called a limiting reality. Our persistence and creativity isn't challenged until we are faced with something or someone who tells us that we can't. At that point, our imagination seems to dissipate. Most children have some goal or dream they want to accomplish. We frame this through the continuous question, "What do you want to be when you grow up?" You will find that some almost instantaneously blurt out an answer, while others stare in shock for like 30 seconds. The reality is some children just want to just make it out of their current situation.

This was my testimony. I grew up watching my mom put in long, hard hours at two jobs. She did everything she had to do to make sure I could have both needs and wants. Because my biological father wasn't as active financially as desired, she pulled double duty to make sure I was taken care of. Thank God He sent her a husband who helped with a lot of that load. He stepped in as "dad," and worked just as hard. I am forever appreciative of that.

Because of this, I knew I wanted a job that allowed me to both help people and make a lot of money. I wanted to make enough to get anything my mom and granny ever wanted or needed. At a young age, I aspired to become a medical doctor. From there, I looked up what I had to do to make this dream a reality. I wrote out what classes I needed, what schools I was interested in, what grades I needed to make, etc. I knew I could not just speak these words, but I had to write them out to review them and stay focused.

One thing about making plans is realizing that they can change. It is okay to make changes to your plan, but always have a plan of action. Because I am a thinker and analyzer, I normally have plan A, B, and C. Sometimes this is good, and sometimes it isn't. Surround yourself with people who will keep you accountable to accomplish that which you have set out to do. Accountability buddies help you to stay focused and recalibrate when needed. Connect with people who are making moves and achieving goals. Why would you want someone who is stagnant to hold you accountable? And guess what, they won't hold you accountable because they are not accountable to their own purpose. Have a plan and figure out the people and resources you need to carry out those plans. It's okay to ask for help and it is okay to make adjustments. If you have a plan and visually review it often, you can accomplish any task you set to accomplish.

Usually at the end of a year or the beginning of a new year, groups of friends get together to have what are called vision board parties. Here you quest through magazines, searching for anything that connects with your vision and spirit. You collectively place these images and words on a poster board and hang it where you can see it on a regular basis. Some people even revisit these around the June/July mark to make sure they are on schedule. For me, I create plans and vision boards according to birth years versus calendar years; meaning I set goals I want to accomplish before my next birthday. The vision board may be complete in one year or these items may reappear on the vision board for the following year. Either way, this is a good way to keep your mind in a place of growing, achieving, and making things happen in your life. It is easy to get into a routine and not realize how fast time is passing you by. Try your best to create deadlines and stick to them. Even if your vision takes a while, know that it is never too late for it to come to pass. You can do anything you put your mind to! With God, all things are possible.

Legacy Scripture: And the Lord answered me, and said, Write the vision, and make It plain upon tables, that he may run that readeth it. For the vision is yet for an appointed time, but at the end it shall speak, and not lie: though it tarry, wait for it; because it will surely come, it will not tarry. - (Habakkuk 2:2–3).

Legacy Builder: Some people write out their goals and visions when inspired while others must schedule planning days for the year.

Which path works best for you?

What dreams/goals do you have in your thoughts that need to be out on paper? How do you plan to bring these to pass?

15

WELCOME CHANGE & ADJUSTMENT

One of the most uncomfortable things in life is change. Change is inevitable. Change doesn't always feel good, yet it is necessary. No matter how hard we try, we cannot stand in the way of change. People around us change; we change; circumstances and situations change. So, since we know this happens to everyone, why not have a plan? Now, I know we cannot block every change that comes, but we can control our reactions or responses to change. There is no sense in having a pity party when things don't work out as planned. Take a deep breath, encourage yourself, and write out an alternate plan of execution.

When our first son was born, I decided I would give nursing a try. My husband and I had a system. I would nurse and pump during the day and he would bottle feed at night with the milk I pumped. It seemed as if we had a plan worked out where we could achieve getting rest with a newborn. My husband was working full time and I was a full-time student while on maternity leave from my full-time job. Little did we know, our son would not take a bottle. Every time we tried to feed him with a bottle, he screamed and cried. It even got to the point where he would cry at the sight of a bottle. There was no choice left but to continue nursing and pumping around the clock. I found myself utterly exhausted.

Rather than brainstorming and coming up with a new plan of action, I became very upset and frustrated, not with our son but with the situation. I also became upset with my husband and envious when he slept. I felt like I was up all day and night, and I wanted just a few hours of sleep myself. Looking back on it, that was not a valid reason to be upset, although my feelings were very real at the time. He was working all day, and so was I with the baby and school; however I should know more than anyone that these bodies will tap out, whether you try to or not.

After reality hit me and I mentally got focused again, I decided to purchase a series of bottles: different brands, different shapes. I knew something had to work. Beyond needing to get rest, time was ticking for me to return to work. What would I do then? I had to figure something out. Because parenting does not come with a manual, I had to learn that I could not be the person to give our son the bottle. It had to be someone else. I didn't realize that the kid was a genius at the time. Why take your supply from an alternate source when the main source is holding you? That is a message right there!

I had to keep trying and not get discouraged. I had to keep pumping and building up my storage as I knew that, even though it was not being utilized at the moment, the time would come for it to be used. During this season, I had to work harder with school to get ahead on assignments and stay up while my son slept to put extra time into pumping, but I had a plan and I had to see it all the way through. I was walking by faith! Little did I know, plans were about to change once again!

My granny was gracious enough to relocate to Dallas with us for a few months after our son was born. As a new mom, it was hard trying to find someone I could trust, so she unselfishly came to be with us. By the time our son was four months, my husband had secured a job promotion back home in Memphis, TN. Unfortunately, at the time, I was still in my time commitment at work and could not relocate immediately. It was my granny and I during the week and my husband on the weekends.

My, was this a trying time. It felt like I was back at square one! My granny had my son all day while I was at work, and though I was exhausted from work and studies, I could not find it in me to ask for help at night. I was nursing, pumping, studying, writing papers, taking exams, packing up our home, and taking care of our son at night. My pride and consideration would not let me express my frustration or the fact that I was overwhelmed.

The weekends when my husband would come would seem to fly by and, to be honest, seemed like they were filled more tension than anything. Something had to give. We were grateful for the promotion, but we knew that we had to depend on God to work a miracle on our behalf. We dealt with change, we adjusted our situations; however, this seemed completely out of our hands. God is just like that sometimes. He will get you to a point where you have no choice but to rely on Him and His plans for your life. The way He works things out is totally different from us, and if you try Him, He will put you in situations just to see how strong your faith is.

Your dilemma may not be like ours, but I am sure there are things in your life similar to this situation. We all have plans. We all have a mental map of how things should work out, but the truth is it doesn't always happen this way. We must welcome change and adjustment, without getting off focus. Change is inevitable. It comes without warning sometimes, but as long as we stay in tune with God, trust Him with our plans, and consult Him on the next steps, He will lead and guide us according to His will. Don't be afraid of change. Welcome it. Embrace it. Because you know the Source and the main One who maps out the blueprint for your life.

Legacy Scripture: Trust in the Lord with all thine heart; and lean not unto thine own understanding.

In all thy ways acknowledge Him, and He shall direct thy paths - (Proverbs 3:5–6).

Legacy Builder: What areas in your life are on hold because you did not come up with an alternate plan of execution?

When change comes, how do you deal with it and adjust?

16

SOMETIMES LETTING GO IS THE BEST OPTION

We never want to end a situation on a bad note or feel as if we have "failed" in certain areas of our lives. Broken relationships is that area for me. I have a slight separation issue. I don't do well with death, nor do I do well with ending relationships or friendships. I am much better than I once was, but I am still working on this aspect of my life.

"To everything there is a time and a season." This applies to relationships as well. Everyone we meet in our lives will not be with us always. Unfortunately, some who were close in one season of our lives may not be as close, or even present, during other seasons. God uses things and people to help us grow, mature, and push through situations. When their time and season is up, it is actually more dangerous and draining to try to hold on to them. Not being able to "let go" can cause more harm than good, especially when bad situations have to force you to walk away.

Letting go does not only apply to people and situations, it also applies to expectations. We all have expectations for things and people in our life, whether we realize it or not. One of the hardest lessons I am learning is how to let go of my expectations in some areas. I did not say settle, and I did not say lower my standards. Expectations affect more than just the person who has them; they also affect those that feel as if they can never live up to them. To you, your expectations may be common sense, general knowledge, consideration, or common courtesy, but to others it may just be another hurdle they simply cannot make it over. If your expectations are causing you continuous frustration, unfulfillment, and irritation, the best thing to do is let it go.

Does letting it go make you weak? Absolutely not. It actually makes you more mature and aware. The situation may not change, you may never get that dream job or even that perfect relationship, but you do not have to hold others hostage trying to achieve your mental goals. Let it go. Walk in your purpose and watch that be the answer to your prayers and bring you more joy than you ever imagined. You may not like your current situation, but I promise if you pray about it, let go of the frustration and expectations, and change your outlook, it will help you to be focused on what matters.

If relationships do not work out, forgive, let it go, and move on. Even in dealing with work, church, or extracurricular items, change your perception and attitude towards the situation, change your response to stimuli, and watch things turn around for the better. All because you let it go and focused on what was important. Trust the times and seasons. Be in tune with God to recognize divine connections, to understand the relationships you should fight for and those you should just let go.

Legacy Scripture: Be strong and of good courage, so not fear nor be afraid of them, for the Lord your God, He is the One who goes with you. He will not leave you nor forsake you - (Deuteronomy 31:6).

Legacy Builder: What situations do you need to let go of?

What expectations do you have in life and of people that are leaving you more frustrated and upset than happy and fulfilled?

What can you do to project your expectations inward versus having unspoken outward expectations of others?

17

BUILD YOUR BRAND

Your brand is what you stand for and what you are known by. Your brand, just like your character, is everything. There are certain standards that come along with building your brand and allowing others to learn who you are. How you represent yourself is evident in the people you hang around or associate with, in your appearance, your attitude, etc. The statement, "The perceptions of others are their reality," has some validity. We can't control how others view us in all cases, but we can affect the crowd that advocates for us.

Regrettably, we live in a society where people will believe the worst about you before they believe the best about you. In conversation with a few friends, I have found out about situations or accusations that happened about me but I was never made aware of them. When I asked why they never said anything, they simply said, "That was not your character." Do you have anyone who can advocate for you whether you are around or not? If someone said I did something or they heard of something out of character for me, my brand, my character, how I carry myself should help/aid in determining whether that is the truth or not.

Make sure you are taking the necessary steps to build your brand. How do you want people to speak of you when you aren't around? What do you want to be known for? These are questions you answer when building your brand. Surround yourself with people who will pour into you, assist you in your growth, and push you; also have those who will correct you when wrong, give you feedback, and help you get back on track. Both areas are imperative to where you need to go.

You can build your brand in countless ways. Start a blog, create your own business, or find a way to impart and change lives. It doesn't have to be anything expensive or super time-consuming. It could be something simple to show you care. Encourage others, take time to build relationships and pour into those you can impact. Also, pay attention to those who look up to you. There is nothing worse than being hurt by someone you truly looked up to and admired. It kind of crushes you so to speak. Be a light. In building your brand, you begin to build your legacy. Much like dominos, the impact you have on one person's life can touch countless individuals, and they in turn will continue to pour into other people. It is truly a beautiful sight.

Sadly, there will be individuals who won't like you, who will try to tarnish your name and your brand just because. There could be something inside of you they wish they had. Maybe there is an aspect of their lives where you took a leap of faith and they did not. You cannot concern yourself with these individuals. Yes, you can try to have a direct interaction, where they can have a first-hand encounter with you. After that, if they still wish to tarnish your name, your brand, and what you stand for, move on. Don't allow stumbling blocks to become distractions and get you off course. Stay focused on God, your purpose, and His will for your life. Pour into others, build your brand, and leave a legacy.

Legacy Scripture: And whatever you do or say, do it as a representative of the Lord Jesus, giving thanks through Him to God the Father. – Remember that the Lord will give you an inheritance as your reward, and that the Master you are serving is Christ - (Colossians 3:17, 24).

Legacy Builder: What is your brand?

Are others aware of what you stand for?

What steps do you take to build and continue to revise your brand as you grow and mature?

18

POUR OUT TO BE REFILLED

Over the years, I have been blessed to obtain countless words of encouragement, helpful tools, and words of wisdom. Naturally, I am a listener. I internalize what is being said, mentally take it apart, and analyze it. It brings me joy to learn from those who have experienced life and care to share pitfalls that I could avoid. I have a heart and passion for sitting with seniors, asking questions, and gathering their words of advice, strength, and reassurance that I can do anything. My spiritual mom has a saying, "I want to die empty, hollowed out," and ever since I heard it, the statement has stuck with me. In that moment, I realized that I had been selfish. I had been taking in, and taking in, but not willingly pouring back out. Whether it was due to my nervous nature or the fear of not being received, I realized that I had inadvertently sat on a lot of wisdom.

Some of the greatest inventors are noted as the greatest simply because they took a leap of faith, regardless of what anyone thought. If the idea did not work, they would go back to the drawing board; but if in fact the idea did work, they had struck gold! If they did not take the leap, the simple thought in their mind would not have produced that multi-million-dollar company.

The truth is we all must leave this earth one day. We cannot take our ideas, wisdom, and desires with us, so why are we clenching them to our chests and guarding them with our lives? Now, I do not mean blurt out those ideas that are still in the works. Sometimes moving in silence is the best. I mean, if you see others trying to do or accomplish things you have already accomplished, lend your advice and resources. If you have more than enough, be willing to give to those who could really benefit from it. Sometimes even pouring out your time can be seeds sown for someone investing in you later down the road.

Unfortunately, you will have those who take your good intentions the wrong way. Do not allow others to speak evil on what you attempt to be good, and don't be distracted by their unwelcoming thoughts. You know you are pouring into others and giving back, one because you have been blessed to do so, but also because you know your season to receive is coming back around. You can't allow everyone and everything to pour into you; however, your relationship with God and sense of discernment should help you decipher what is the meat of the meal and what are the bones you are to just spit out and keep it moving.

It is also important to note that pouring doesn't just occur from person to person. There will be times when God Himself will pour His wisdom, knowledge, revelation, downloads, witty inventions, creative ideas, and just more of His spirit! All are necessary. Look at all of the examples in the Bible where God literally poured out of Himself on others. We have to make sure we are in tune and in a posture to receive from Him!

Legacy Scripture: I pray that God, the source of hope, will fill you completely with joy and peace because you trust in him. Then you will overflow with confident hope through the power of the Holy Spirit - (Romans 15:3).

Legacy Builder: What are some areas in which you could clear the clutter or pour out?

Start with your clothes and then write out ideas that you have been holding on to.

Are there any individuals that you could pour time, advice and resources into?

19

DON'T ALLOW REJECTION
TO DISTRACT YOU

Rejection is no respecter of persons. Everyone has experienced some form of rejection at some point in their lives. We have all heard the word "No." No to jobs, no to ideas, no to new opportunities. Just No! Of course, I have spoken about my journey to medical school several times in this book. School after school, advisor after advisor said, "No," "Not Right Now," "You just aren't good enough to compete." Hearing this over and over again devastated me and threw me into a cycle of confusion and depression. This was all I have ever wanted in my life, and somehow I never factored in the possibility of me not getting into medical school and achieving my goals. I knew if I got in, I was set and would finish. But I never factored in never making it that far.

I am not going to act like I did not cry, get depressed, and feel completely lost. I'd entertained the thought of other careers before but not with any real depth or intention to follow through. I knew that I could not stay in that place if I was going to make something of myself. I would have to refocus and redirect my thoughts and expectations. More than that, I had to seek God for my purpose: His plan for my life. One thing I knew for sure, those Nos would eventually turn into one Yes.

Distractions come to get us off focus, to get us all in our "feelings," and to slow down our momentum. Being productive feels amazing. Why? Because you are tapping into your destiny and what you were created to do. When rejection comes, just thank God that He has something better coming. It may be a no for now, or there may be an alternative planned that is better suited for your life down the road. Why not trust the One who knows all? Take that opportunity to pray that God will give you a vision of what path is right for you in this season. If you allow rejection to distract you, you could be missing out on valuable time.

Rejection hurts. Rejection is unexpected and scary, but guess what. God is right there with you to lead and guide you. Am I a medical doctor today? No, but I work for an amazing company with good pay, benefits, and a retirement plan. I know that if anything happens to me, my children will be taken care of. So, while I was rejected from what I thought my heart wanted, though I was rejected from the only occupational future I imagined for myself, God had other plans. And in that, I have learned to trust Him with my heart, my desires, and my ambitions, all of me. He alone is my heart's desire and being in His will is the ultimate goal. Who knows, something may come about and bring me back full circle in the future. Sometimes a no is a not yet. Keep praying, keep pushing, and keep working; God will lead and guide you to exactly where you need to be.

Legacy Scripture: For I know the thoughts that I think toward you, says the Lord, thoughts of peace and not of evil, to give you a future and a hope - (Jeremiah 29:11).

Legacy Builder: In which areas of your life have you experienced rejection?

How have you allowed your emotions and thoughts resulting from rejection to distract you?

What can you do to get back on track?

20

BE INSPIRED TO INSPIRE

When my time comes to die, will it matter that I even lived? This is one question I ask myself all of the time. God has placed so much potential in all of us; what a shame to leave this earth still holding on to it. I want to pour out everything that I have in me and also share those very tools and principles I have obtained along the way. I want to inspire and be inspired.

Have you ever come into contact with someone who inspired you? Someone who made you feel like you could do more, be more, strive for more? That is called being inspired. It is important that you surround yourself with people who inspire you and push you beyond mediocrity.

One of my best friends runs a six-figure business. She inspires me daily to do more with my life. Though our circumstances are different, she takes the time to pour ideas and share nuggets that can help propel me to where I want to be in every aspect of my life. The goal is for us all to inspire each other. I have friends who I admire that are in the medical profession while they are inspired by my ability to be a mom and wife, working full time in corporate America. You should be inspired to allow your life to inspire others.

Whose life have you poured into? What wisdom have you shared? Are you open, willing to give knowledge freely, or are your hands shut tight, not wanting others to beat you to the top? We don't exist in this world just to drift through life on a daily basis. We are here to impact lives and affect change in the world. Find out who inspires you, what inspires you, and go after it! We never "arrive" in this life, so don't ever get to the point where you don't aspire for more. Envelop yourself with people who are doing something with their lives—gather wisdom from those who are where you are trying to be. These people will stop at nothing to make sure you are walking in purpose. Don't be content with floating through life. Don't just exist, Be! Be someone who is inspired to inspire.

Legacy Scripture: Let love be without hypocrisy. Abhor what is evil. Cling to what is good. Be kindly affectionate to one another with brotherly love, in honor giving preference to one another; not lagging in diligence, fervent in spirit, serving the Lord; rejoicing in hope, patient in tribulation, continuing steadfastly in prayer - (Romans 12:9–12).

Legacy Builder: What inspires you?

Do you seek to inspire, impact, or influence?

How do you plan to do this?

21

SELF-CARE

We all have that one area of our life that we just have not conquered. Self-care is that area for me, and I am actively working on getting better at it. I am great at making sure everyone else is taken care of, finances are in order, business is handled, but I always forget one major piece of the puzzle: myself. I am starting to realize that if I do not take the time to care for me, I won't be any good to the very people who depend on me.

Some people confuse self-care with being selfish. Others can try to make you feel guilty for taking a moment for yourself and for stepping back to get a fresh look and perspective on your life. We can find ourselves in a constant routine, especially as parents, and look up and realize that life has seemingly passed us by. We have given and poured into everyone else while neglecting those things we wanted to do for ourselves. Don't let this be you. Write down your dreams, set your goals, form a plan of execution, and get it done. Yes, things and circumstances can get us off track and even shift our timeline a bit, but do not allow your desires to get thrown away. You are important and you are worth the time it takes to be great.

At the end of my pregnancy with our second baby boy, 38 weeks to be exact, I had to take a day, one night to myself. I knew that our lives were about to drastically change, growing from one child to two, and I was already mentally, physically, emotionally, and spiritually depleted. I needed a moment alone. I made arrangements for my son to be with my mom and informed my husband of my feelings. I expressed that I needed to recalibrate, rest, work on my book, and just self-care. We all needed it. He needed a moment away from me and our son as well to get himself prepared for our new normal. It is okay to take a step back, as long as you all are on the same page and in agreement.

I did a few things to pamper myself, checked into a hotel, and simply rested. That night was needed, and I realized that taking the time to focus on me for a change helped me tremendously. Not only was I able to be more present with my family, I also got the physical and mental strength to birth our second son the following week. Take care of you so that you can care for those who depend on you.

Self-care is necessary and required in order to be successful. Avoid burnout and frustration by taking time for you; that is after you spend time with God and in His Word. Time for yourself is not limited to rest or doing something nice for yourself. This also includes investing in tools that better you as a person, whether it is coaching, reading books, or continuous education, whatever helps you to be a better you. If that means remaining knowledgeable and relevant, do that. If you won't take the time to pour into yourself, what makes you think others will? You cannot build a legacy if you aren't physically able. Self-care is necessary for survival. Start today.

Legacy Scripture: Give all your worries and cares to God, for he cares about you - (1 Peter 5:7).

Legacy Builder: What is your self-care regimen?

When is the last time you had a self-care day?

How do you end your nights and reflect for the next day?

What you can do better?

CONCLUSION

It is not easy to be transparent. It is not easy to let the world in on your journey: the good, the bad, and the ugly. One thing I have learned over the years is people connect with the heart and what is real. If my story has helped just one person, then it has all been worth it!

My goal was to motivate you, empower you, and, most importantly, ignite a fire inside of you. My goal was to reassure you that no matter what anyone says, you can rewrite your own story. It does not have to mirror that of everyone in your family. You can, in fact, break the cycle and create a new normal.

Regardless of the past or what you have done, despite the hurt, disappointments, and losses, you can create your own inheritance—your legacy. Do not let anyone trick you into thinking you are not qualified for this assignment. Believe it or not, you are more qualified than most. If only you could see yourself through the lens of God! Hopefully now you can!

We all have a purpose to fulfill—a footprint unique to ourselves that we must leave in this earth. Do not allow your clock of life to stop before you have left your indelible mark. You were created by God to impact the world, and now you have been equipped to do so. Take the scriptures and reflections that you have journaled while reading this book and go build your legacy.

You are a change agent. A trailblazer. A trend setter. You are the author of your life's story, and you can set the trajectory of the generations that are to come after you. You have been challenged. You have been motivated. You have been empowered. What are you waiting for? My legacy began with ME and now you... Be Blessed is my prayer!